THE NEXT IN LINE

DATE DUE

Demco, Inc. 38-293

THE NEXT IN LINE

CHRISTOPHER SCHMIDT

WINNER OF THE 2007
SLOPE EDITIONS BOOK PRIZE
SELECTED BY TIMOTHY LIU

SLOPE EDITIONS
NEW HAMPSHIRE | NEW YORK | MASSACHUSETTS

Published by Slope Editions
www.slopeeditions.org

Library of Congress Cataloging-in-Publication Data
Schmidt, Christopher, 1975–
    The next in line: poems / by Christopher Schmidt—1st ed.
      p.cm.
    ISBN 0-9777698-3-6
    I. Title

Book design by Christopher Schmidt
Printed in the United States of America

X X X X X X X

FIRST EDITION

I am grateful to the editors of the publications where these poems first appeared, often in different forms:

Butt: "Top/Butt"; *Court Green*: "Go Lightly"; *La Petite Zine*: "By the Sea," "Callas Benched," "host body"; *The One Three Eight*: "Priapus Met"; *P-Queue*: "Love Machines"; *Tin House*: "All Tomorrow's Parties," "tenement."

I am honored and grateful that Timothy Liu selected these poems for publication. I want to thank the folks at Slope Editions—Ethan Paquin, Christopher Janke, and the indefatigable Jeannie Hoag—for their support and patience. Douglas A. Martin, Whitney Lawson, Jason Schneiderman, and especially Barry Disman offered invaluable help in the book's production. Above all, I am grateful to Wayne Koestenbaum, for his example and his encouragement.

The excerpt from Mark M. Anderson's *Kafka's Clothes: Ornament and Aestheticism in the Habsburg Fin de Siècle* is reprinted by permission of Oxford University Press.

Contents

I. THE NEXT IN LINE

II. ARCADES PALARE

III. LOVE MACHINES

Introduction

The Next in Line situates paradise in the future, if not the immediate future, then at least in the possibility of a future, a poetry that privileges the Barthesian striptease over the present tense of the flesh. The Past is a bust. Nostalgia is a luxury this Poet finds difficult to afford. Maybe Freud was wrong about childhood as the exclusive source of happiness, about the overrated pleasures of repetition. Where then to set up camp? These poems make their home in anticipation rather than gratification, Mr. Schmidt's satisfactions rooted in the end game of delay in a world where secrets must remain secret. Eschewing the candor of a daytime talk-show host, his muse is more like a chanteuse in a Berlin cabaret, covered in feathers and blood. And whether one prefers to stand in line or on line, perhaps you too will find, as I certainly did, that this first book was worth the wait, number after number holding me in thrall as I wondered just what might happen next…

TIMOTHY LIU, *November, 2007*

for Leif Larson

I. THE NEXT IN LINE

All Tomorrow's Parties

Expect no takers. Don't hate Queens.
Where everyone is smoking
is and is not here. Lumberjack
stares at the boyfriend, the boyfriend.

Serious? Serious? Like interns
on TV. Like, fun. Another malady.
Cat and mouth and cant and mouse.
My sentiments exact.

Swallow, stumble
pie could not but sweeten
in a saucer, tarter saucer.
Dress mine with lime, with lime.

Each one blows the next in line.
Had I courage, I'd warm the others.
Night-night the only greasing.
The wind troubles me also.

Go Lightly

Helen chooses beans and egg whites. June:
yogurt, prunes. "Starch can line a skin like stress,"
says Helen. June: "I bloat a tide full moon."
Sugar is not a vegetable, "ought" a thing to obsess

about. Sunday and sleet, the sisters fast. Icings snake
in a spun sugar glade. (Organics moot?)
Pastries are their butter sirens. Cake—
epithalamial—is eyed, deemed "beaut,"

"non-beaut." Elegance is refusal, said Garbo.
Said Vreeland. Said Hepburn. The roleplay
between them gets very intense. No Capote hobo
mouths "Lulamae" to spoil their *Roman Holiday*.

Treacle is to Equal as Tiffany to rhinestone.
Stories up, breakfast, above the Hudson's brine cologne.

Avoids
(Beckett Essay)

In English, said it was "too easy" to write poetry. Wrote in French and no Poems.

When Peggy tried to stay the night, ran from his own room so quickly He.

Some couples: Vladimir / Estragon. Mercier / Camier. A / B. Listener / Reader.

A: I could stay like that for ever, with my head on an old man's knees.
B: Knee.

Kafka at the Black Party

Kafka, and thus the aesthete in general,
oscillates between self-denial and self-display.
MARK M. ANDERSON

Some things about you aren't Prague at all

An aquarium of ice

Probably the squirrel skating branches

And the pattern of emulsion

The fan you couldn't tell if slowing, skinning

Even the trees aren't leaving yet

You see the stereotype, black on white, nail it

A manifold curing

Like Christ, a pose in twists enacts

"Only with such an opening . . ."

His lantern jaw, like liquid, ripples

The pines so furred, spiked ruffs at neck

Crop-caught, you allure: "pleats, frills, and appendages"

Too long for its weakness . . . a tailcoat discussed

host body

At the side of the garden, an appendix of rhubarb, mysterious, perennial. She hums with the organ. Of the mucosal stomach lining, wines disabuse his folly. The minister hands his tissues over. That article, my bible. Scissoring legs punctuate the caucus. Sundays, she remembers broken palms on the boulevard. "They ran their hands right over." Ream empty, it takes a pillage. Evangelists envied the tyrant's blank stage. Others decried. As I did, Ed died.

tenement

what makes pigeon
pigeon? I must know

what makes him
pick my window

wrought escape
dirty opening

keep his murmuring
from my sleep

worries his
sorry nothing nest

tethered to zero
why not fly?

pigeon! I say
I grab him round—

his feathers my fingers
catch in prayer

a shriek breaks
his hollow breast

a new sound yet
still so pigeon

so throttled
so lame

his moldy eyes
roll to the sky

nervy thing
his larded wings

leave my hands
dark as newsprint

Kafka at the Bathhouse

You wanted free of father, faster.

a look not yes, not no

Stuck a finger in—and it was good.

heart-trumped, awkward at the turnstile

Asters arrest you beyond the ghetto.

the pool not discouraging

You'd die to stand in line. No foyer meant no push.

a tenor neither usher

Max entered first, then you did.

costive, you saw horrors, honors

a labyrinth of cabins

the TV's caffeinated wink

like melons couched in thighs

flock the humid prison

lashes spiked like type

And what touched you most?

The poet in you could egg cocks,

buoy them to poignance.

"Don't forget what you came for."

or sex, at best, a wet concussion?

Brod, as though finished
hiking the dark side
of a wooded peak
assumes a martial posture.

"As you were."

fathers   daughters

no abacus   no calculator   the game
the system   my *tante* taught me
aged 8   (the copy editor in me)

caduceus?   caducity?   the left paw holds
a tally of five   the right hand fans
hemiola   (hearts)   I and aunt account

at grandpa's   town principal   bar tender
all knuckle–die   and third lip best
I associate with pipes   dignity

"Indians from the rez" don't   nor she
Karen Ann   second daughter   from realms
of coin   of "glamour"   —Scot for *spell*

Georgia

Your "price check" echoed.
We all egged too hard.

Burrito the game
you loved too much to play.

Opposite the airshaft
we wondered what you'd see.

The day you broke with
"Daddy's house is messy."

Mommy left Cher
and curtains for you.

Versus

Tumblers in a lock. Coulter of a plow. Moldboard, share.
Rather farmer than father. Tractor cabin a crystal coach, driver
imprismed. Hired hand. Brain fire only slough can quench.
Tractor then an octopus, skittering lateral over fallow. Too
young to drive. High time to bale. Then damp harvest and
how to pay. The problem begetting lever, machine. Give me
a log tong, I'm good.

Hard G

Came late to the lesson
and played exercise two.
Then the piece in 3/4 time,
strange name, G-i-g-u-e.

"Gig-ew!" Perry laughed
when I said it.
"Gig-ew!" The room
narrowed to my temples.

Perry studied sax
in Paris, France,
had cards printed with *rue
du* something on back.

Is that where he learned
tight jeans, long hair
and not to mind
his skin was sandpaper?

Now red from laughing:
"Shit, don't be sour, kid."
Saxes swabbed, we lugged
them to the parking lot.

In front of his pick-up,
he tagged my shoulder,
shook his head,
and said, "Gig-ew"

one last time. Drove off,
girlfriend his passenger,
and never told me how
to say it, his secret.

Multiple Choice

Fe/male?
In 2006, New York legislates sex as elective, fluid, gray.

> A gray matter.
> A matter of gray matter.
> The matter between ears, not legs.
> Not that pink matter.
> Not that it matters.
> It doesn't matter.

In 2006, New York changes its mind.
Dis/proving its point.

Block Text

Black. Black letters. Blackhead. Black Island. Around the black. Black the scene. Black the quarterback. Jenny from the black. Cell black. Cockblacker. Block dick. Big block buck. Back in block. Pitch block. Block Attack. Block Panther. Block Power. Blockface. Block Letter. Block.

inter

dying to untell how

one keeps a skin on

the bag we may never wish

wrinkled   pursed   unclear

no inbreeding in my line, no

Orpheus coerced performs

the French pronounce without

the desiring mind at rest is why

end   story   conception

countertenor encounters

of course not uniquely for

alarm mediates pleasure as

our age of entourage brings

the eventual sex of

ball bearings to mind, do you

release as if cinching

no dress rehearsing

no drying *Miercoles*

without watching first

Code Sore

Or, prepositioned.

Flint a language
that can't be revised.

Lines under ours.
Ivy on the couch.

Each character bussed
& ampersands sewn on.

Birthplace: marked.
Age: a bad password.

A dog stopped with tales
worrying a bit.

Sonnet

He's tiger, I'm stripe.
He's book, I'm sleeve.
He's the record, I'm the stopwatch.
He's slop, I'm pig.

I'm sleeve, he's green cardigan.
He's face, I'm nose.
He's pucker, I'm cheeky.
He's pluck, I'm rose.

He's sanguine, he's humor.
I'm solo, they're gang.
He's bangers, I'm mash.
I'm schedule, he's train.

He's natural, I'm parable.
All's tale, we're told.

Accommodations

On Arrival

Dank words coined for this
like hall-smells-urine, geranial.
"This edifice at the intersect
of East and West."
Beaux Arts? More like arsenic.
More like arsenic. *Nragggh.*
In fact I'd rather rot.
Peats please, must we?

Project Lobby

We wake to Sandor's liquid fast.
Vodka-swimming cube to skew
our sights, seeing. Eye of camera
catches sex, watch. *Hungary?*
Here's a brunch of proems I brought.
Magyar yoghurt.
Runny honey stuffing
entreating punctuation
and fattening at that.

KM Saga

The synagogue holds us to smocks.
I think of lice and light bulbs
I'd coat with papier-mâché
then smash the Adam in.

Project Lobby II
I lobby hunt. This sinks
in once whine takes root.
We're princes minus kingdom
but kind of mean, you know?
Coupled with a fear of heights
vertical and alcohol.
Gellert funicular.
The language I find granular.
This burns, this tips it.

In the Spirit
Nights, ghost tanks
roam shaded streets
whose quiet is possessive.
Window yawns, scrim indrawn.
Off the forest coverlet!
Clear the soiled doily!
In a strong dark
rim me in Communism.

II. ARCADES PALARE

Blue, Lit, Special

Slapstick, oddly, a *comedy*.
Blue connoting *dirty*.
The paint a bugger to get off.

Outside Target
J snorts coke
in Roxy state.

Inside, we shop
the boys section
—for sizes, not pulses.

Club and commerce:
1. Tight fits.
2. Arena space.
3. Thin light.
4. Discards.

Science of _____.
When butt is bumped
less apt to buy?

a) Sex. b) Shopping.
Optic. Toxic

raptures.

Arcades Palare

Woke up bruised, fruit that I am. Prepare a drink called
Ultimate Meal. It does not assist suicide. Nothing to do in
January but write, with movies so bad. Someone whistling
Rod Stewart. Maybe a little sexy. Fall in love with a saint.
Winter in love with summer. Spring left to its own devices and
fortunately never rusts. The man who fell to mirth. Improve
your Flash skills without a trench. Want ads. To go away.

Top/Butt

Born of sunlust, bus runs to sub-Boston porn moor, horny homo zoo. Looks stun. No frumps, no fops, just buff studs burnt brown. Luc, uncut, hunts cut cock. Jock, hung, lucks on smooth boy cunt, round rump up on dun outcrop. Coy youth sucks thumb, sub for schtup. Jock's pud pulls north. Jock stubs youngun's mouth, swoons. Put out, Luc ducks bud's fuck. (Luc's wont: most lust.) Soon Luc spots humongous chub on pup slut Todd. Luc's succubus guns. Our two gods mushroom. Todd pulls Luc's hood. Luc flops Todd, rubs Todd's rump, drums Todd's knot, churns Todd's rut, tugs Todd's butt. Thus room, sucks nuts. Todd grunts, tough to bottom. Luc lobs sputum up Todd's duct: unctuous. Todd succumbs. Luc mounts, pounds Todd's dog. Bum rush! (No condom?) Todd pouts, Todd coughs. To Luc: Too rough! To Todd: Shut up! Crowds form. Luc pumps, pulls out, punch-fucks: Wow! Luc undocks, spurts globs of ghoul grub (cum) on buns. Luc's spunk, cock drop south. Dusk. Luc glows, Todd numb.

Arcades Palare II

Almost at mother's breast I began assimilating. "We're cold," they
moo. "Because we're so low-fat." Stomach's rusted, needs a muffler.
Coat slicked with oil, neck choked with rainbow. Duck! Do your
heels hurt from spurring? Do your brains hang low? So chapbooks are
gay books? Artifact: reverse the slide from books to chaps. You do the
math. He posed with an amphora covering his bits. He posed with
anaphora covering his bits. Woman is a ruins; we stalk the peristyle.

The Tapestry Takes Precedence

Allergic to . . . statement?

Dust motel.
Clean crib.
Steel frame.

I am too happy, she says.

Firs before pine. Skeins before purls.

(The bird would like to know if
canary or just . . .)

Have longings, though, thawing.

Material culture.
Mother tongue.

Division of the what and how folks.

Weft, toast to a t.

A Little Learning Is a Profitable Thing

The old school advertises its advertising class. The new school advertises *in* its advertising class. Corporate execs sponsor assignments, then shadow-watch as pupils sell themselves the wares. Teachers' branded pets, your continued tuition is appreciated.

Unprofessional

In the pedagogical arena
you can't advance predict

who will learn,
who will teach.

Teach a man to fish,
reject horse gifts.

Teach a man to teach,
expect horse gifts.

*

Nathan, one of my students, has horns. Not real
ones—curls of hair he twists when he's thinking. It's
charming, I don't know what it means. He wears a
button on his vest that says, *Hit Me*. Smart, because no
one does. Freaks the kids out.

*

The actress Marcia Cross has said, regarding her work for the
television serial *Desperate Housewives*, "Sometimes I feel like I'm

being paid not to eat." A trenchant observation that I would like to extend globally. Consider profession not as action, or talent deployed, or time purchased. But as constraint. The contractual suppression of an aspect of subjectivity. Hunger, say, or curiosity. When I began work for a corporation, I was given a book, *Don't Make Me Think!* I quickly realized this was a job description. Not to provoke thought: the summit of my supervisors' expectations. Yet it was a tricky contract to uphold, as it directly contradicted a mandate of my previous profession, teacher.

*

I was hovering over Nathan, helping him with a problem set. He was flicking some eraser dust off his paper when something slipped out of his hand. For a second I thought it was his eraser. Or maybe a wadded tissue? It was a finger, an extra one. A half-digit attached to his pinkie with this isthmus of skin, this strand of integument. He let me get a good look at it, then he flipped it back up into his fist. When our eyes met, he blushed. But there was also this little smile on lips, like he was pleased. Like the whole thing was planned.

*

The prostitute paid not to admit boredom.
The teacher paid not to admit boredom.

The prostitute paid to sacrifice her time.
The teacher paid for time she compels others to sacrifice.

The state may pay for the boarding of teachers.
This is called a hiring bonus.

The state may pay for the boarding of prostitutes.
This is called jail.

*

I saw Nathan standing in front of the school
arboretum. I asked him what was the matter. *Waste
matter,* he said, and snorted. *No, seriously, I could use
a ride home. Can you spot me a ride?* I paused, waiting
to see if he was joking again. Tough cookie all of a
sudden. Finally, emotionless as possible, I said, "Where
do you live?" *Just past Salt Hill,* he said, twisting his
horns. *Actually, I don't live there, but if you could drop
me there, that would be cool.* "OK," I said, "that's on my
way home." He didn't ask where I lived.

*

Who manages the poet? The whips of some twenty-six serifs lash her. Form speaks, deranging profession. *And just what is it you do?* I stretch myself till the line breaks.

*

I started the car and put it in reverse. Mudhoney
on the dial. My gaze on the rear-view mirror when
Nathan said, *You know my secret now.* I braked, looked
down. His hands were open, cupped together as if
lifting water from a well. Except no water. And there
they were, cinched in the crooks of his pinkies like
tight little grubs—the extra fingers. "Oh," I said. I was
surprised. Surprised I didn't know better what to say.

*My mom says that my dad had them too. But he had
them cut off before she knew him. I don't know why I
don't get rid of them, but I don't want to. Is that weird?*

*

In ancient Greece, sex, instruction on intimate terms. I've heard
unlikelier pairings. Science and shit, it's said, share a root.

*

Office hours. Nathan came by to pick up his final project: portraits of his hands as sine waves, with the sixth finger marking the gap between sine and cosine. It was really good. He brought another boy with him—older, maybe a college student, maybe a drop-out. Fierce kid with tattoos, a little faux-hawk. Acted like he had the whole scene cased. Both of them were wearing these self-satisfied looks, like they were onto something radical. Some new discovery. It seems like that the first time. "Great work, Nathan. Really fine. I'm a fan."

au bureau

chased that buck
with a shot of *something*
to get the john off

undercover directive:
direct   treat   meat
what pound means?

when pleasure is business
no leisure no bed woulds

Not in Kansas

The Queen made by screaming queens a sentence few would write. Those who know, don't. Those who care, scare. The queen waves with queenly bearing. Queensberrying (like bunburying, like Ashberying). Some queens hate borough queens. Some queens hate queeny queens. Motherfucking explaining queen. Queen's day v. queen for a day. Queen of hearts v. queen of spades. Diamond queen. Club queen. Dairy, rice, chocolate queens—quinoa queens? Drama queen but poetry queen? Size queen but time queen? Proust queen but Melville queen? Queenqueg? Queers query queens. Queen queries, these. Queenqueeries.

Arcades Palare III

Proms pose. A room of hard ones coming at me like
submarines. In her water routine, skimmed over me like a
potboiler. Coupons. When asked if Ute sang "Ich bin ein
Vamp," seemed depressed to say yes. Leaflets bag fleas. A
frought train caught in shorts, as in Hitchcock. Film strip as
a verb. All personalities too strong. Sour mouth says much.

By the Sea

What kind of sauce is by the sea?
Sticky dog-eared pages by the sea.

Merman man. Peters town. Lansbury.
Vocalise memorial in "By the Sea."

Stein to Alice: "Baby, let's be regular."
Finding bottom nature by the sea.

Sweet sweat pages. Shore ode's
genius perspiration by the sea.

Marie betrothed from Austria:
I've been to paradise but never by the sea.

EuroDisney draws out the incontinent.
Mickey leaks on Goofy by the sea.

"Pat prefers beaches *and* mountains."
Darling no such thing as by the sea.

I Alone

Dans ce monde, il faut être un peu trop bon pour l'être assez.
MARIVAUX

Every toad wants a piece.
Mr. Irresistible.
Gotta swallow it.

In the locker room
I wear a sign
to cover my ass.

Says, *Sorry*
boys, taken.
Seems to work.

Every poet knows
he's lousy.
Me? I'm the shit.

Cock of the walk.
Talk of the gown.
Knotless wood.

Almost too good.

The Last Shangri-La

I had to sue Tibet.
When they red-carpet-tossed
me down K2

skeins of saffron yak thread,
needles still attached,
stuck me in the back.

I recovered in a kidney
infinity pool.
The view killed.

The food stank.
Just thicker-skinned, I think.
Bigger boned. Just. So. Great.

Buddhist, but maybe they could consider
the consequences of their actions.
A little, like, *live in the moment.*

I'm telling you—I'm boring you?
You've seen the reenactment on TV?

Better, more moving
in my tell-all memoir,
at Book Soup, $14.93.

Priapus Met

You are carved, and sex
so gross, so dunk me god.

Ever poise on
chattel, marble.

Disease
you give new gloss.

Hamstrung?
Quiver!

Malfeasant putti
(fauns so wrong?)

push buttons, noses.
That smarts!

Thought spoils over?
Enter England, empty, hounded.

No Romeo, but soft
would not befit you.

At least you're "partnered."
She's kept her bust, and little but.

The stadium about the head,
odd knots, and then the girding?
She's sewn them,
most sub rosa.

Arcades Palare IV

Check letters have jaded bottoms. A poke, a pep pill. Master of the nonsequitur. Little zinnias born minus sin. Tissue culture under attack. What matters the titer sounds grim. Chilling rebuke, champagne. The translator missed her target language. A poem of lines and lies might seem trite. Tarmacadam suspected of superficiality. Bring "jakes" out of the water closet. Not a catnapper by any stretch.

Callas Benched

She held court at the Met, but we couldn't figure out which one. Missed her. Damned her. Professor suggests we convene seminar there in tardy vigil. Yet can't catch the echo of her high E-flat—too many earphones, art phones, chatty cicerones who wish they'd studied law. Grandeur, Ebay sells your carcass with lipstick traces on the pipe mouth. Legal? No. Platonic? Learning is a dialectic with isotopic synthesis. The more cavalier the teaching, the more I learn. To be cavalier. On Klavier. Class dismissed.

Pencil Me in at Two?

At the pitch meeting for an opera
called "Diaspora"—aka disaster—
we'd accounted for betrayal, sovereignty, waltz.
It was practically writing itself.

Get her, said Bob—ol' Bob Wilson—
looking much the Mapplethorpe still.
(Was it the lighting, arranged in advance?)
He was pointing at a headshot

with chopsticks. Debate raged.
Who'd work? Who'd *had* work?
The libretto was stained with coffee.
It was practically writing itself

into the piece. Then I saw my opening.
I'd cut out, hit the gym,
be back by lunch. After I left, Bob
was pointing out the headshot

of a lapsed acrobat cruising me
right then at the stretch station.
Or maybe just pushing a sitcom.
"It's practically writing itself,"

he boasted, bending back my legs
into a deep, key-lit V.
"When can I show you my talent?"
He was pointing at his headshot.

Invitation to Ms. Kiki DuRane

Makebate in plush fakery, flirt in comfortable coral
pants suits, diva-in-decline in training (sans train),
take these words of watching, stay your leaving,
> *please come flaming.*

Dramamine queen, hairpin hostess of "Sophoclean rage,"
award a foxy dollar, yourself another CC and Ginger (sponsors beware).
I see you as the Electra–Hecuba–Medea of East 13th street & Avenue AA.
> *Please come flaming.*

Imaginary pearls you trade you for swine
of us: paint wardrobe a comedy of manners, upstage
Mizrahi, sincerity (easily).
> *Please come flaming.*

Keep your cool babysitter. No, take your cool babysitter
and mind the gap between her there, Kiki here.
Defuse boy drama, refuse false buoying,
> *please come flaming.*

The first to nail Miami muscle Marys rehearsing Christmas pageants
at the gym, saccharine silicone teens who dare to bore.
Never show minus face, pitchfork.
> *Please come flaming.*

Drop your *mise*(ry)-*en-scène*-making. You're better chewing scenery.
Swan your way to Faery retreat, or stay and pound with me
these stinking streets. Opine if manhole covers are extinct,
> *please come flaming.*

Snub obvious beauties, snobbery, *Sex and the City.*
We will die for, will die for, will—won't beg for Mary or Dusty.
Maybe a smidge of Momus but never, never Madge.

Queer Jesus, join your Judas audience
for a kiss and tell and tell and tell.
Admit, spirit arsonist, you miss us, and
   please come flaming.

Fire Island

Gabby men on the next blanket
flirt through magazines. Another couple
matches a white baby to its toys.

A sandy dog spots his owner, naked, part
the surf. We watch from the boardwalk,
ignore the man when he passes.

A doctor, prominent, erects his net
for volleyball in a Speedo, in a fit.
His the best deck on the beach.

If rare, must this be paradise?
How real estate scrubs our camp
of charm. I don't appreciate. Does any body?

> *So we should sell while high.*
> *So we should buy while cheap.*

The poet on the ferry back
looks too much like his lover.
Says my lover, takes our picture.

Making Eyes

Ground, white.
Then hole for light

the size of why
not a pine nut?

Go with two.
One goes blank,

you've got your
spare

& parallax fixes
lazy ones.

Render edge
of obscure moon

an index
of spectrum:

gem rims,

softens the
eclipse.

III. LOVE MACHINES

A poem is a small (or large) machine made of words.

WILLIAM CARLOS WILLIAMS

I want to be a machine.

ANDY WARHOL

Love Machines

YouTube swells the ranks of screen gilds. Self promotion graphics expose phallus, assonance, big time. Fame games, machine dreams expand band width. Net sex cast broad, why return to skeletons, pole roles? Thin, skin so uninteresting.

*

Laptop, brain on their wavelength. Outside firewalls, my mind a dry book. Pages fan. Charged ions lifting hair, I think. En route to the corner library, I wade the radio currents of my own fossiled thought.

*

Since they magnetized the sidewalks, a rash of deeds, deaths. Air conditioners coaxed from throats. Fire escapes escaped. House numbers dropped like stocks. Belts, braces, pacemakers brought us to cobra, mouths wet to the nickel. Got in touch with our earth. Worshipping the ground. They walk on.

*

Robot sex: clock in, tick off. Their means of reproduction—a command performance. Even their spare parts attractive, like batteries. Laws prevent human–robot contact: stick to like. Odd. In our culture, it's difference we legislate.

*

Were you inhibited as a child?

Inhabited, like a mobius strip.

We've seen your autoerotics.

In congress with your surveillance.

How did you know our gaze?

I felt my pleasure as vector.

You can't escape a mobius.

I wrote "puberty" and grew new dimensions.

We long to experience unreliable self, to feel "fat" when not.

Isn't your "we" by nature labile?

We know too precisely its contours.

Forget edge. Unteach. Become.

*

The museum of unnatural history. Old machines lever age. Bots that bought it, bytes that bit it. Their story mirrors ours: rounded corners succeed sharp edges, avant-garde. A hunger for the modern. Just feed us the Dada.

*

Sisyphus the first machinist. A hard drive up grade. Crash. Reboot.

*

Taught me the efficiency of additive difference in a binary set.

Taught them the beauty of the blinking green cursor.

No wingding like meaning.

Could we be depressed?

The chips are down?

We feel nothing.

Never weather?

Bored.

Pre-tends depression.

Its square root?

Its square rot.

Return to subject!

Subjection not subjectivity.

Don't push our buttons!

I see no buttons to depress.

*

{ - - }

I pitch "reality" TV. The Ghost in System. Add bulb to nose. Jelly to belly. Horn to crown. Take form, derange.

{ + ? }

Like rust to duct. Unplasticize. Make hemispheres tricameral. Render $1 + 1 = 3$. Wire left to left, catch prat-fall, laugh. Har-har.

{ + - }

Grab skein of veins and let her rip? Inject botulism with a little humor. Bile best.

{ + + }

Fine flaws my premise promises. My cruelty they value.
The hazards of flesh a gas.

*

Mooning around titanium. Iron desire. I fell for a silver spoon in my mouth. Hard, the metallics of love.

*

In my hard drive, we semiconduct the whole unspeakable affair. Hangs on my every word. Just my type. Responsive to my touch. Even my palinodes she saves as rich text. Lost our connection on politics. Silicon, I should have guessed, conservative by nature. In nature, facetious.

Favorite film?

We're very interested in Persona.

Bibi or Liv?

Liv's emotional efficiency impresses. All she a/effects with blank.

And Bibi?

Brilliant deployments of glass shard, face cream.

Hold a sec—checking email.

We're assigning them to you as analysands.

But I analyze only in bed.

Also twins amalgamating your erotic predilections.

Big nose, fake tan, big nose, fake tan?

We asked them to simulate a wilding.

Careful, I have poems in incubation!

Master Trope

Mechanically, the poem most axle-like.

Gains in pinion force what's lost in distance traveled.

Revisionary ratios: a mad hand circles words, knots excess to the rack.

Imagined readers crank the invisible handles.